EXTREME U.S.A.

Lisa Trumbauer

CONTENTS

Rigby®
A Harcourt Achieve Imprint

www.Rigby.com
1-800-531-5015

U.S.A., COUNTRY OF EXTREMES

To be extreme is to push something to the limit. The word *extreme* is often used to talk about sports like BMX biking, cliff jumping, and skateboarding. These sports are totally extreme, but there are lots of other things that can be extreme, like the people and places of the United States.

There are things in America you can't find anywhere else in the world. We have extreme sports, but we also have extreme hobbies, extreme buildings and structures, and extreme weather.

You're about to discover everything from the sweetest place around to driest place in America. You'll also learn what a storm chaser is and who discovered the deepest cave in the country. Do you know where the tallest rollercoaster in the United States is? Find out inside *Extreme U.S.A.!*

Many Americans enjoy extreme BMX racing, extreme skateboarding, and extreme . . . pumpkin growing!

3

Chapter 1

EXTREME CITIES

New York City, NY

Which U.S. city has the largest population?

The city with the largest population is the "city that never sleeps"—New York City. This city has just over 8 million people and is made up of five boroughs, which are like very large neighborhoods. These boroughs are called Manhattan, Brooklyn, Queens, Staten Island, and the Bronx. Each of these boroughs alone has more than one million people, which makes New York City like five cities in one.

Central Park is one of the most popular places to visit in New York City.

During colonial times, New York City was called New Amsterdam. It was also the capital of the United States for several years during the American Revolution. Today, the city has several nicknames, including Empire City, Gotham, and the Big Apple.

What draws so many people to the Big Apple? Many people who live here say they couldn't imagine living anywhere else. Along with the cultural and historical sites, New York City also has large parks, several zoos, and loads of shopping. It also offers many different job opportunities to people from all walks of life.

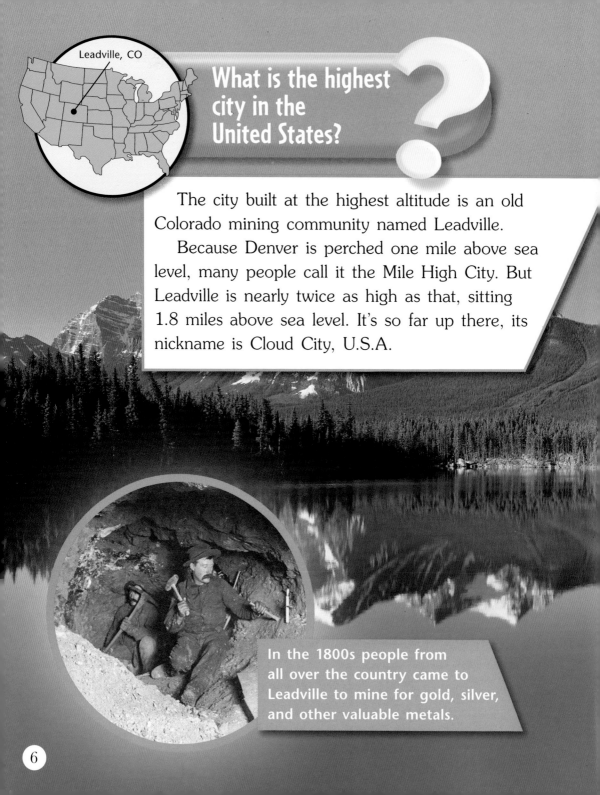

Leadville, CO

What is the highest city in the United States?

The city built at the highest altitude is an old Colorado mining community named Leadville.

Because Denver is perched one mile above sea level, many people call it the Mile High City. But Leadville is nearly twice as high as that, sitting 1.8 miles above sea level. It's so far up there, its nickname is Cloud City, U.S.A.

In the 1800s people from all over the country came to Leadville to mine for gold, silver, and other valuable metals.

Originally a mining town, Leadville is now a popular tourist site.

Unlike many western communities, Leadville did not start as a cowboy-and-cattle town. Instead, people here made a living by mining. Many people came to Leadville during the 1800s in hopes of making money working in the silver mines.

Today, almost all of the old mining camps around Leadville are closed, leaving behind empty ghost towns and forgotten signs of the past. If you ever decide to visit, be on the lookout for old pick axes and lost nuggets of silver!

Hershey, PA

Where is the "sweetest place on Earth"?

Welcome to Hershey, Pennsylvania, a city made famous for its Hershey brand chocolate.

The city of Hershey is filled with factory tours, a theme park, museums, and even a zoo. Street lights in the shape of chocolate *Kisses* run up and down Cocoa and Chocolate avenues. More than 2 million people each year visit Hershey's Chocolate World, where they see first-hand how chocolate is made.

Chocolate inspectors watch the chocolate bars pass by, making sure that every piece is perfect.

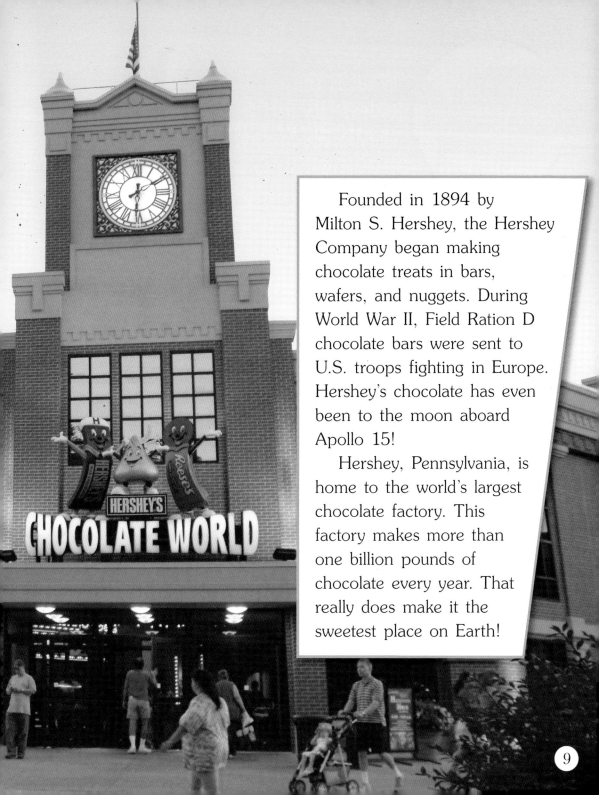

Founded in 1894 by Milton S. Hershey, the Hershey Company began making chocolate treats in bars, wafers, and nuggets. During World War II, Field Ration D chocolate bars were sent to U.S. troops fighting in Europe. Hershey's chocolate has even been to the moon aboard Apollo 15!

Hershey, Pennsylvania, is home to the world's largest chocolate factory. This factory makes more than one billion pounds of chocolate every year. That really does make it the sweetest place on Earth!

St. Augustine, FL

What is the oldest city in the United States?

More than 440 years old, the city of St. Augustine, Florida, is the oldest city in the United States.

A small city with a population of just over 12,000 people, St. Augustine was founded by Spanish explorers who reached the Americas on August 28, 1565. Since then, five different flags have flown over the city: Spanish, British, French, Confederate, and American.

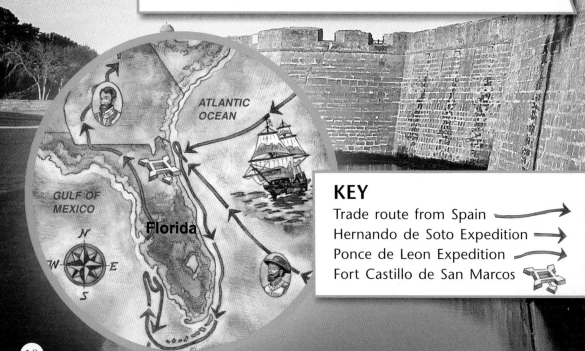

ATLANTIC OCEAN

GULF OF MEXICO

Florida

N
W E
S

KEY

Trade route from Spain ➝
Hernando de Soto Expedition ➝
Ponce de Leon Expedition ➝
Fort Castillo de San Marcos

During the 16th century, the Spanish built a fort at St. Augustine called the Castillo de San Marcos. This army base protected the settlers from pirates, such as Sir Francis Drake, who wanted to rob the Spanish of their gold.

The Castillo de San Marcos still stands today, and the Spanish culture is still very important to the people of St. Augustine. The Colonial Spanish Quarter is a living history museum, which means that actors and tour guides dress in costumes of the Spanish colonial period.

Chapter 2

EXTREME NATURE

Death Valley, CA

Where is the hottest place in the United States?

America's #1 hot spot is Death Valley, a desert in southern California. This area is hot all year round, but on July 10, 1913, the thermometer hit 134° Fahrenheit. That's the hottest temperature ever recorded in the United States.

POTENTIAL
FLASH FLOOD
AREAS

NEXT
40 MILES

Signs warn visitors of
the danger of flash floods.

It may seem strange, but even though Death Valley gets less that two inches of rain a year, there's still a chance for flooding. This is because the ground is so dry that when it does rain, the soil often cannot soak up the water.

The water all runs down into the valley and can become very dangerous. In fact, people die every year because of these sudden flash floods.

Tornado
Alley

What area of the country gets the most tornadoes each year?

The American Meteorology Society, a group of scientists that study the weather, have named the central part of the United States "Tornado Alley" because of the high number of tornadoes that strike these states every year.

Tornado Alley stretches from Texas up to North Dakota, which puts a lot of people at risk. Tornado winds can reach speeds of 300 miles per hour. These dangerous storms can last for hours and can travel more than 100 miles. About 60 people are killed by tornadoes each year.

Every year, tornadoes cause millions of dollars in damage to homes and property.

Weather scientists and storm chasers study tornadoes so that we will be better able to warn people in danger.

Storm chasers must be quick if they want to see a tornado up close. They watch the skies above Tornado Alley, and when news comes that a tornado is forming, they drive as fast as they can to the spot so they can gather scientific data. They often have to drive hundreds of miles just to catch a glimpse of a tornado before it dies out.

Rockefeller Forest, CA

What are the tallest living things in the world?

The Coastal Redwood trees in California are called the tallest living things in the world. This species of redwood tree is know as *Sequoia gigantea*, which means "giant sequoia," or the "big tree." The tallest of these redwoods is over 360 feet tall and thousands of years old. No other trees in the world grow to such heights.

The hole in the Chandelier Tree was carved in the 1930s. It is six feet wide and nine feet tall, which is just large enough for a small vehicle to drive through.

These trees are so tall that the tops are often struck by lightning. This can be a serious problem, especially if a fire starts 150 to 200 feet above ground where forest rangers can't reach to put it out.

Rockefeller Forest in California holds forty of these redwoods, the most famous of which is the Chandelier Tree. This tree is so wide, a hole has been cut through the center that is wide enough for a small vehicle to drive through.

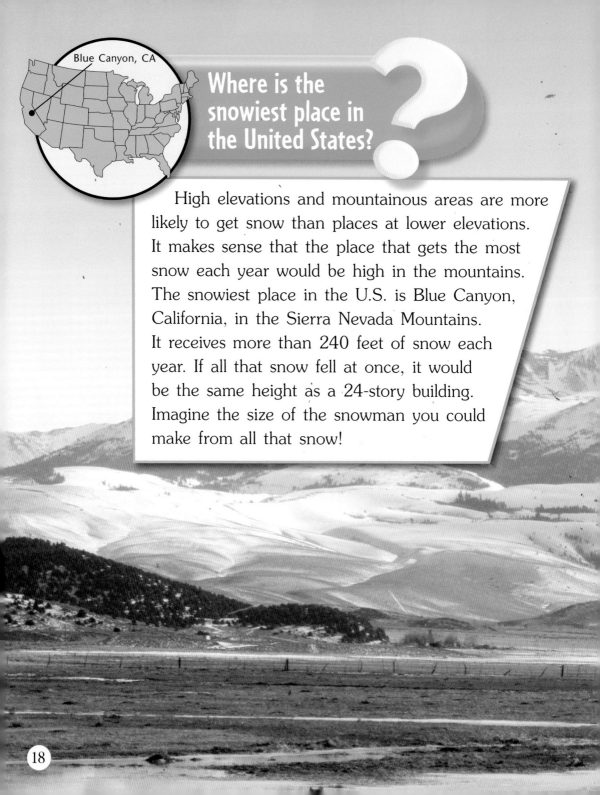

Blue Canyon, CA

Where is the snowiest place in the United States?

High elevations and mountainous areas are more likely to get snow than places at lower elevations. It makes sense that the place that gets the most snow each year would be high in the mountains. The snowiest place in the U.S. is Blue Canyon, California, in the Sierra Nevada Mountains. It receives more than 240 feet of snow each year. If all that snow fell at once, it would be the same height as a 24-story building. Imagine the size of the snowman you could make from all that snow!

Vacationers like this snowboarder love the heavy snowfall in the Sierra Nevada mountains. It means lots of powdery snow for extreme fun!

Other places in the United States also receive a lot of snow. Marquette, Michigan, is in second place for most snowfall with a little more than 128 inches of snow per year. Other states on this list probably won't come as much of a surprise—Minnesota, New York, and Maine. Here's one, though, that might surprise you—Flagstaff, Arizona. Arizona is better known for its deserts and dry heat, but Flagstaff receives nearly 100 inches of snow a year. That's because part of Flagstaff is in the mountains.

Carlsbad, NM

Where is the deepest cave in the United States?

The deepest cave in the country is the Lechuguilla cave in New Mexico. It's so deep that explorers have yet to find the bottom! The deepest part of the cave that's been measured so far is 1,632 feet straight down. More than 101 miles of the Lechuguilla cave have been explored, with no end in sight.

It is one of 80 caves in Carlsbad Caverns National Park, but unfortunately it is not open to the public.

Stalactites are rock formations that hang from the roof of a cave. They often look like huge icicles made out of rock.

Stalagmites are rock formations that rise up from the floor of a cave. They form over thousands of years from water dripping down from the roof of the cave.

The Lechuguilla cave was discovered in 1986 when a group of spelunkers, or people who explore and study caves, wanted to see what was at the bottom of a "bottomless" pit called Misery Hole. What they found was an amazing new cave system stretching deep underground.

Ever since then teams of scientists have found new and beautiful stalagmites, stalactites, and other amazing rock formations. Very few people are allowed into the Lechuguilla cave so that it stays in its natural state.

Chapter 3

EXTREME STRUCTURES

Chicago, IL

What is the tallest building in the United States?

There's one building in America that towers above all others, and that's the Sears Tower in Chicago, Illinois. This skyscraper stands 1,450 feet tall and has 110 floors. Not only is it the tallest building in North America, but it is the third tallest building in the world. It took three years to build and costs more than 175 million dollars.

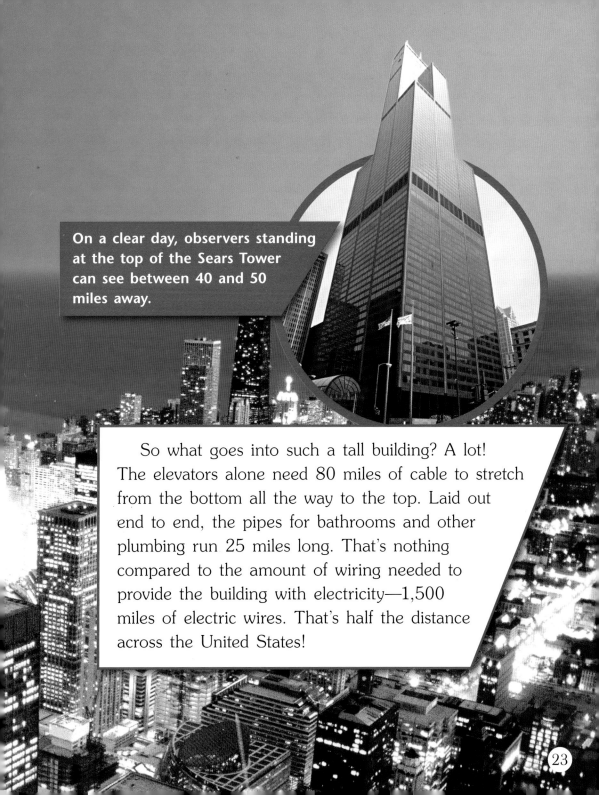

On a clear day, observers standing at the top of the Sears Tower can see between 40 and 50 miles away.

So what goes into such a tall building? A lot! The elevators alone need 80 miles of cable to stretch from the bottom all the way to the top. Laid out end to end, the pipes for bathrooms and other plumbing run 25 miles long. That's nothing compared to the amount of wiring needed to provide the building with electricity—1,500 miles of electric wires. That's half the distance across the United States!

Lake Pontchartrain
Causeway, LA

What is America's longest bridge?

This honor falls to the Lake Pontchartrain Causeway in Louisiana. This flat, concrete bridge stretches nearly 24 miles across the water, connecting the north and south shores of Lake Pontchartrain. It is not only the longest bridge in the United States, it's the longest bridge in the world!

The Lake Pontchartrain Causeway is actually two bridges in one. Traffic on each bridge only goes one way: one bridge goes north, and one bridge goes south. More than 30,000 cars travel over this bridge every day.

Because the Verrazano Narrows Bridge is so long, the builders had to take into account the curve of the earth's surface while they were designing it.

But that's only one type of bridge. Another type is a suspension bridge, which is a very long and very strong bridge. The weight of a suspension bridge is suspended, or held in place, by steel wires attached to towers that are buried in huge concrete blocks.

The longest suspension bridge in the United States is the Verrazano-Narrows Bridge that connects the boroughs of Staten Island and Brooklyn in New York City. This bridge is 7,200 feet long and is named for the Italian explorer Giovanni de Verrazano, who was one of the first Europeans to sail down the Hudson River.

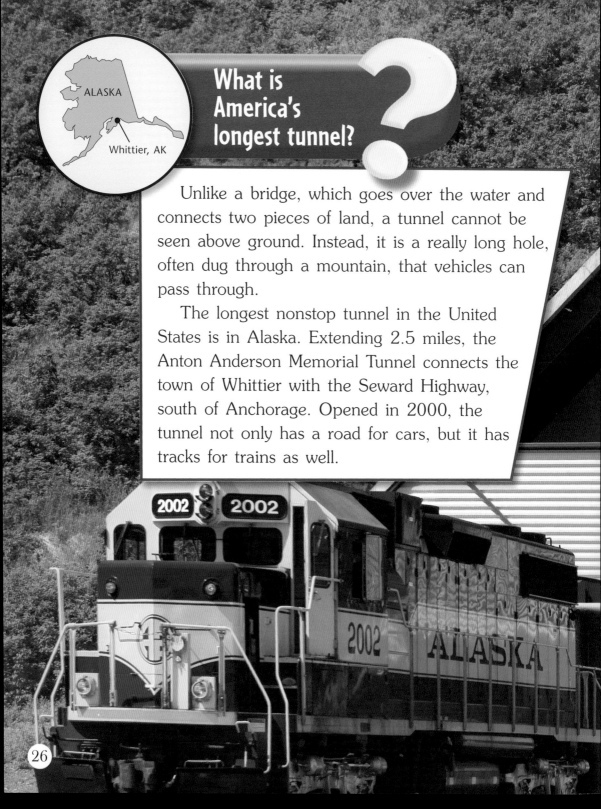

ALASKA

Whittier, AK

What is America's longest tunnel?

Unlike a bridge, which goes over the water and connects two pieces of land, a tunnel cannot be seen above ground. Instead, it is a really long hole, often dug through a mountain, that vehicles can pass through.

The longest nonstop tunnel in the United States is in Alaska. Extending 2.5 miles, the Anton Anderson Memorial Tunnel connects the town of Whittier with the Seward Highway, south of Anchorage. Opened in 2000, the tunnel not only has a road for cars, but it has tracks for trains as well.

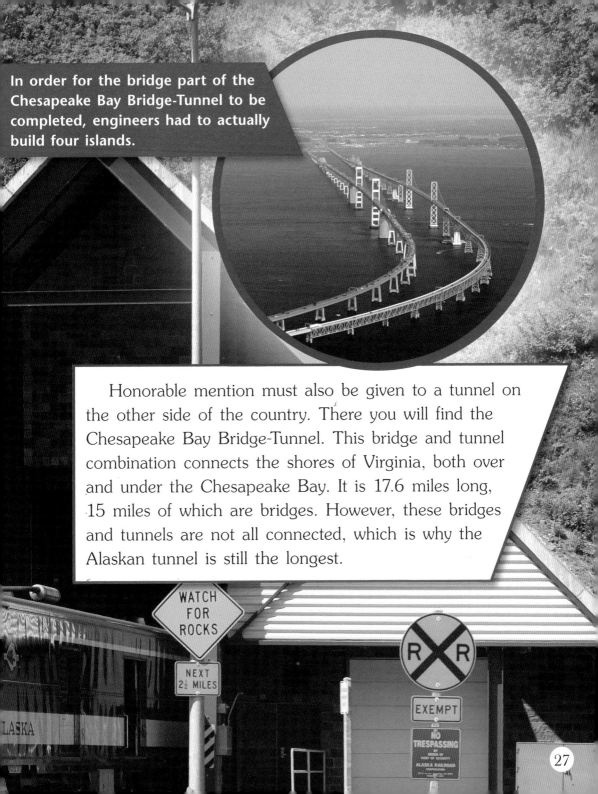

In order for the bridge part of the Chesapeake Bay Bridge-Tunnel to be completed, engineers had to actually build four islands.

Honorable mention must also be given to a tunnel on the other side of the country. There you will find the Chesapeake Bay Bridge-Tunnel. This bridge and tunnel combination connects the shores of Virginia, both over and under the Chesapeake Bay. It is 17.6 miles long, 15 miles of which are bridges. However, these bridges and tunnels are not all connected, which is why the Alaskan tunnel is still the longest.

WATCH
FOR
ROCKS

NEXT
2½ MILES

R X R

EXEMPT

NO
TRESPASSING

ALASKA RAILROAD

LASKA

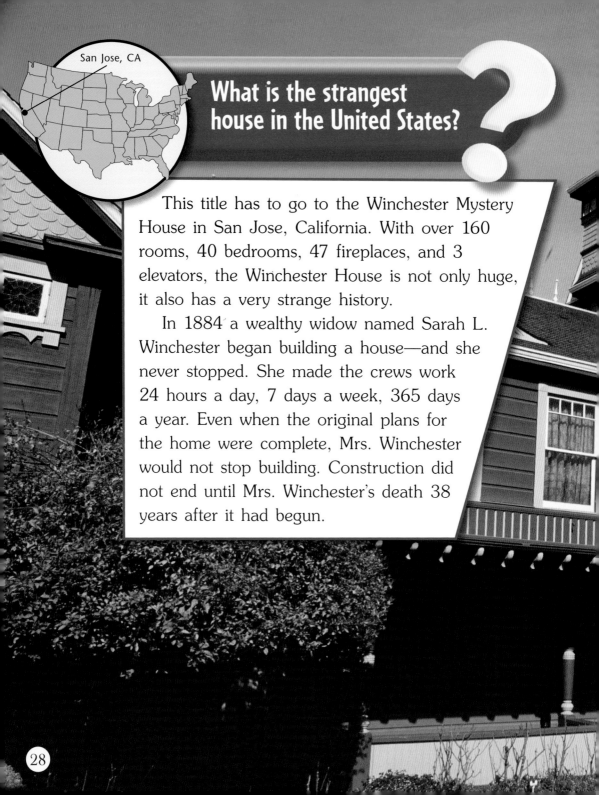

What is the strangest house in the United States?

This title has to go to the Winchester Mystery House in San Jose, California. With over 160 rooms, 40 bedrooms, 47 fireplaces, and 3 elevators, the Winchester House is not only huge, it also has a very strange history.

In 1884 a wealthy widow named Sarah L. Winchester began building a house—and she never stopped. She made the crews work 24 hours a day, 7 days a week, 365 days a year. Even when the original plans for the home were complete, Mrs. Winchester would not stop building. Construction did not end until Mrs. Winchester's death 38 years after it had begun.

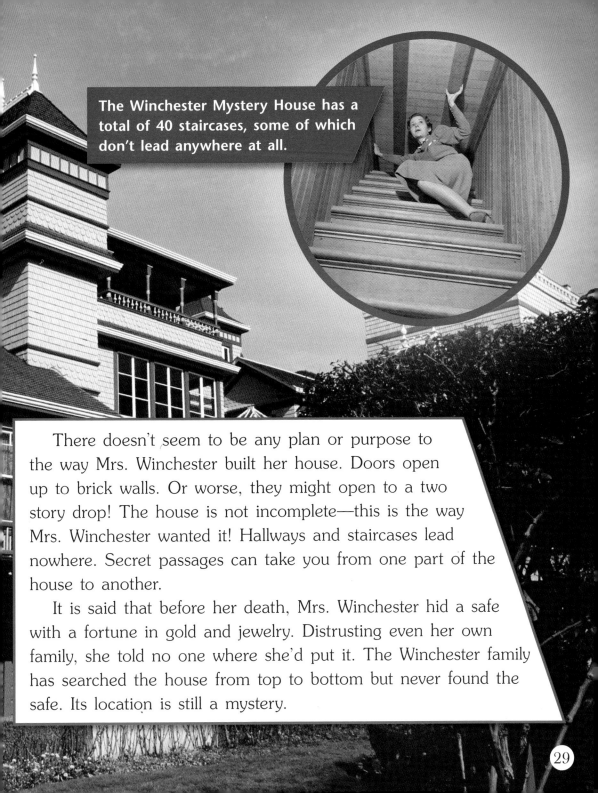

The Winchester Mystery House has a total of 40 staircases, some of which don't lead anywhere at all.

There doesn't seem to be any plan or purpose to the way Mrs. Winchester built her house. Doors open up to brick walls. Or worse, they might open to a two story drop! The house is not incomplete—this is the way Mrs. Winchester wanted it! Hallways and staircases lead nowhere. Secret passages can take you from one part of the house to another.

It is said that before her death, Mrs. Winchester hid a safe with a fortune in gold and jewelry. Distrusting even her own family, she told no one where she'd put it. The Winchester family has searched the house from top to bottom but never found the safe. Its location is still a mystery.

Sandusky, OH

Where is the tallest roller coaster in the United States?

Is 420 feet tall enough for you? That's the height of the Top Thrill Dragster at Cedar Point Amusement Park in Sandusky, Ohio. The ride has the look and feel of a racetrack. The station is decorated with checkered flags and colored banners, and the trains even look like racecars!

After climbing this 420 foot hill, the Top Thrill Dragster plunges straight down! The whole coaster only takes 16 seconds to complete.

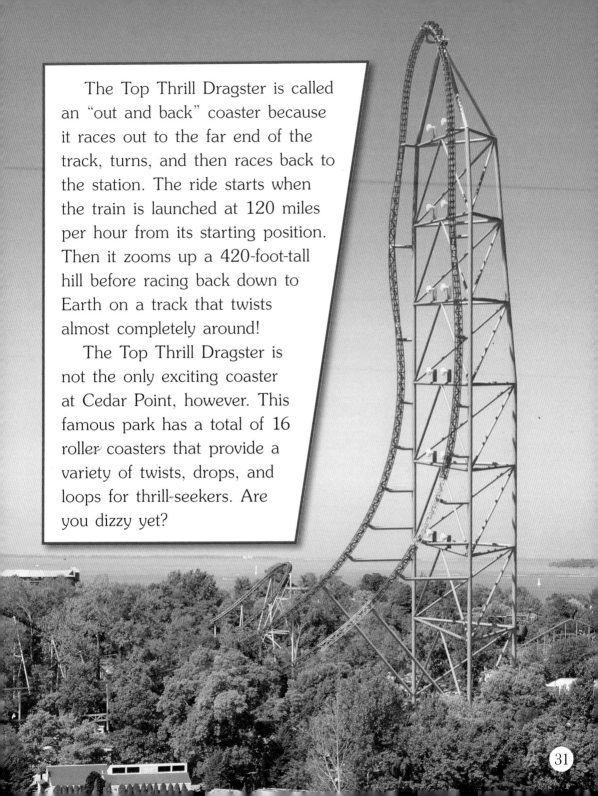

The Top Thrill Dragster is called an "out and back" coaster because it races out to the far end of the track, turns, and then races back to the station. The ride starts when the train is launched at 120 miles per hour from its starting position. Then it zooms up a 420-foot-tall hill before racing back down to Earth on a track that twists almost completely around!

The Top Thrill Dragster is not the only exciting coaster at Cedar Point, however. This famous park has a total of 16 roller coasters that provide a variety of twists, drops, and loops for thrill-seekers. Are you dizzy yet?

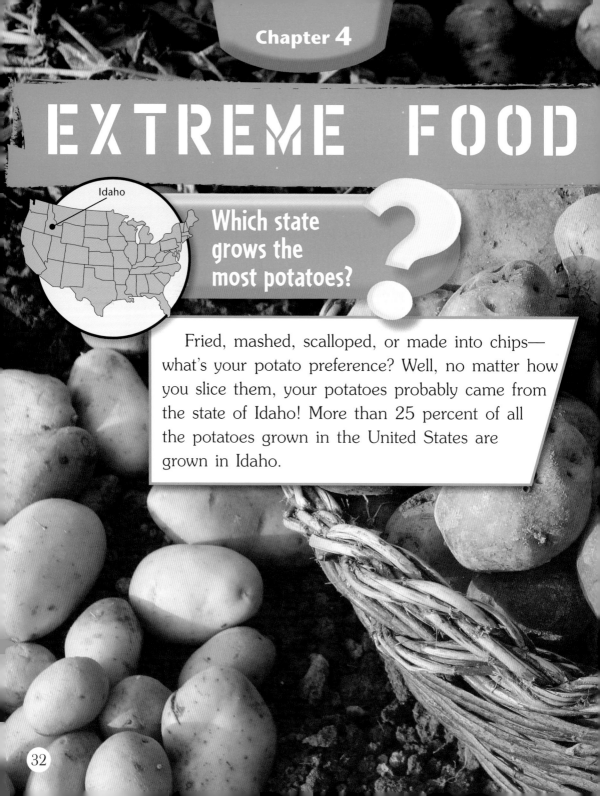

Chapter 4

EXTREME FOOD

Idaho

Which state grows the most potatoes?

Fried, mashed, scalloped, or made into chips—what's your potato preference? Well, no matter how you slice them, your potatoes probably came from the state of Idaho! More than 25 percent of all the potatoes grown in the United States are grown in Idaho.

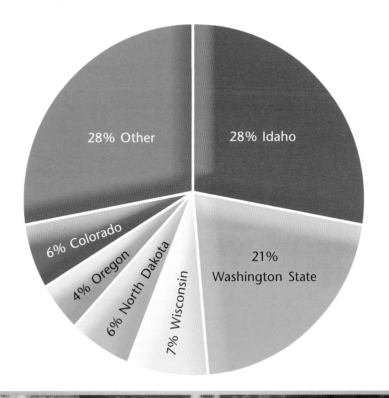

Potato Production in America

- 28% Other
- 28% Idaho
- 6% Colorado
- 4% Oregon
- 6% North Dakota
- 7% Wisconsin
- 21% Washington State

In 2004, the United States produced a total of 20.4 million metric tons of potatoes. That's more than one billion bowls of mashed potatoes!

The most popular Idaho potato is the Russet Burbank, which is great for both baking and boiling. Each Idaho resident would have to eat 63 potatoes every day to equal the number of potatoes the state exports each year.

Georgia

Which state grows the most peanuts?

The U.S. peanut prize goes to the state of Georgia. Almost half the peanuts grown in the United States come from this southern state. Peanut production is so important to Georgia that the peanut is the official state crop.

About 4,800 farmers in Georgia grow peanuts. In fact, a United States president was once a peanut farmer—Jimmy Carter. He was president from 1977 to 1981.

What happens to all of those Georgia peanuts? Many are used to make peanut butter. According to one source, Americans eat about 2 million pounds of peanut butter each year, as well as 1.6 million pounds of roasted peanuts. With 42 percent of all peanuts in the United States coming from Georgia, chances are your peanut butter has Georgia peanuts in it.

California

Which state makes the most ice cream?

One out of every eight gallons of ice cream made in America was produced in the state of California. Of the nearly 1 billion gallons of ice cream made in the United States, around 116 million gallons were made in California.

To make 1 gallon of ice cream, you need about 12 pounds of milk. California produces more than 20 billion pounds of milk each year, or 20 percent of America's milk production.

Americans spend around 10 billion dollars each year on ice cream. That means that this ice cream factory has a lot of work to do!

ICE CREAM FREEZER

California also leads the nation in production of sherbet, which is ice cream made from fruit juice instead of milk. Yet with all the different ice cream flavors out there, the flavor that remains a favorite is still vanilla. Vanilla makes up about one third of all ice cream flavors sold in the United States. Butter Pecan and other nutty flavors are the second most popular. Chocolate comes in third.

Some of the stranger flavors include: cactus, garlic, clam chowder, and sea slug.

GOING TO EXTREMES

You can explore extreme U.S.A. in your own area. Each state has its own extremes just waiting to be discovered.

Copy this list in a notebook, then put together your own *Extreme U.S.A.* book about places that are closer to home. Don't just look for the ordinary—go to extremes!

- What is the highest point in your state? The lowest?
- Which city gets the most rain?
- What was the hottest temperature ever recorded in your state? The coldest?
- Which city has the most people?
- Which city has the tallest building?
- Where can you find the longest bridge or tunnel?
- Which food does your state grow the most of?

INDEX